IF... Bounces Back

IF... Bounces Back

Steve Bell

A Methuen Paperback

For Heather, William, Joe and Patrick

This collection first published in Great Britain in 1987
by Methuen London Ltd
11 New Fetter Lane, London EC4P 4EE

The strips first published by *The Guardian* 1986 and 1987

Copyright © Steve Bell, 1986, 1987

Designed by Brian Homer
Edited by Steve Bell and Brian Homer

Typeset by P & W Typesetters
1489 Pershore Road, Stirchley, Birmingham B30 2JL

Made and printed in Great Britain

British Library Cataloguing in Publication Data
Bell, Steve
  If - bounces back.
  I. Title
  741.5'942   PN6737.B4

ISBN 0 413 15890 X

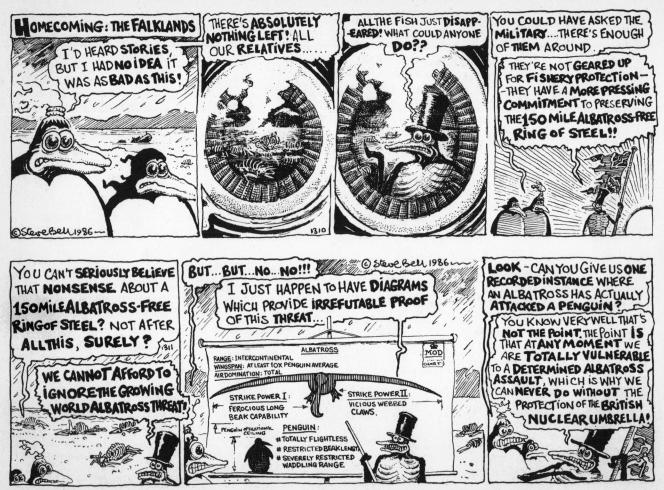

10

11

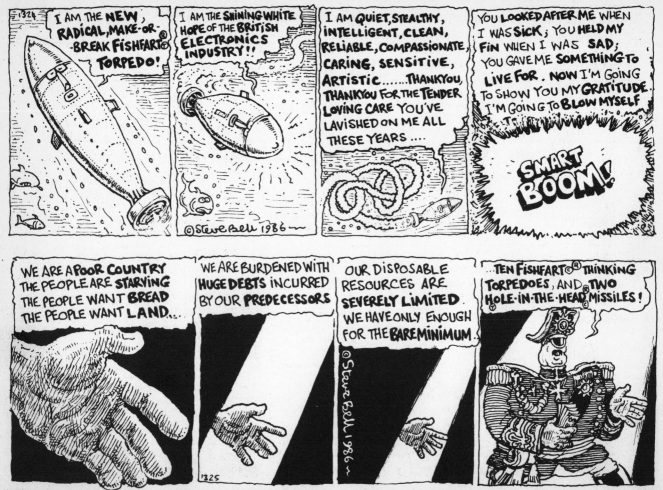

12

14

15

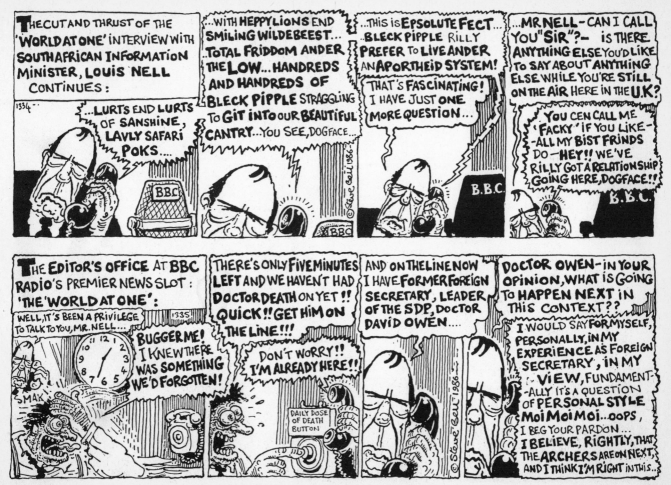

17

18

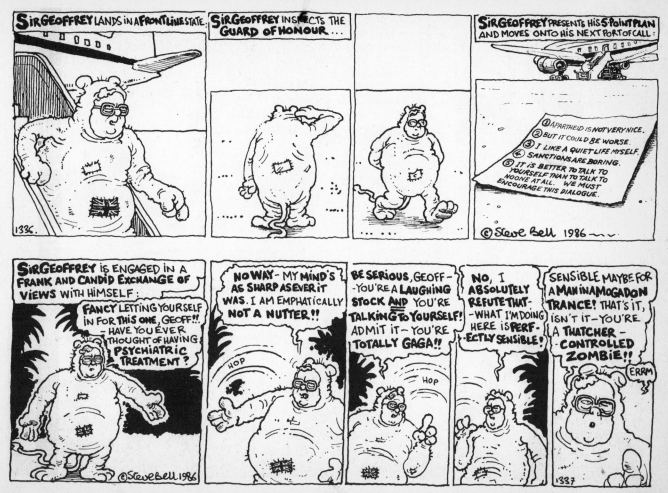

19

21

23

25

29

By LYING ABOUT HIS AGE, HEIGHT AND PERSONAL HABITS, THE PENGUIN HAS GAINED ENTRY TO THE METROPOLITAN POLICE :

HURP TWO, HURP TWO, HURP TWO, HALT! LEFT FACE!!

"COMMUNITY AWARENESS ROLE PLAY BY NUMBAHS!! IMAGINE YOU ARE AN ETHNIC-TYPE PERSONAGE IN A PROBLEM FAMILY-STYLE SITUATION : ONE: "OH DEAR! PROBLEMS, PROBLEMS, PROBLEMS! I'M BRAHNED ORFF IN A BABYLON!"

1358

TWO: "GORDON BENNETT!! I CAN'T TAKE NO MORE! I'M GOING TO GO AHT AND 'AVE A RIOT!!"

THURREE: "CRASH BANG WHUMPA WHUMPA WALLOP!! I GOT THESE PRIMITIVE JUNGLE RHYTHMS POUNDIN' THROUGH ME VEINS!! I'VE GOTTA STICK SOMEBODY'S 'EAD ON A POLE PRONTO!!"

FOUR: "OOMF! SMACK!! LUMME!! A PLASTIC BULLET IN THE KISSER!! I'M ORFF!!!

FIVE: "BACK 'OME AGAIN : THANK GAWD THAT BATON ROUND KNOCKED A BIT O' SENSE INTO ME! I FEEL MUCH MORE ME OLD HAPPY-GO-LUCKY OUTWARD GOING SELF AGAIN! I THINK I'LL WATCH CRICKET ON T.V!!

HENDON: 1986:

WELL, YOUNG PLODLETS: THE ROLE OF THE POLICE HOFFICER 'AS MUCH HEXPANDED IT'S PARAMETERS SINCE THE DAYS OF DIXON OF DOCK GREEN...

NOT ONLY IS THE HOFFICER EXPECTED TO FILL THE ROLE OF SOCIAL WORKAH, RACING DRIVAH, INDUSTRIAL RELATIONS ADVISAH AND STORM TROOPAH; 'E NOW FILLS THE ROLE OF PUNDIT AND POLITICAL COMMENTATAH!!!

SO, 'OO WANTS TO 'AVE A GO AT ROLE PLAYIN' THIS ONE?? YOU AT THE BACK : THE SHORT BLACK + WHITE ONE : CAN YOU DO IT??

YUS: THE REASONS FOR THE DECLINE IN PUBLIC STANDARDS ARE AS FOLLOWS : ONE: -T.V.; TWO: EASY CREDIT; THURREE: THE FAILURE OF CERTAIN LOWER CLASS ELEMENTS TO FIND JOBS;

FOUR; DRUG ABUSE; FIVE: DIVISIVE LEFT-WING POLITICIANS; AND SIX: SIR KENNETH NEWMAN'S MESSIAH COMPLEX AND SQUEAKY VOICE!

1359

HEXCELLENT! MIND YOU - I'M NOT SO SURE ABAHT THAT LAST ONE!

33

34

THIS IS YOUR TRIBAL RIPRISINTATIVE KING SMILING TOM GOODVIBES XXIII. HE'S HERE TO PROTECT YOUR INTERISTS...

HOW EXACTLY DOES HE DO THAT??

© STEVE BELL 1986

IT'S QUITE SIMPLE, MY DEAR, THE GAVERNMINT PAYS ME BIG MONEY TO BUY TOP HETS AND IXTRA BIG DINNERS FOR MYSELF. IF YOU DON'T LIKE IT, I SEND MY BIG BOYS ROUND TO DO YOU UP PROPER...

BUT DON'T WORRY, DEAR - I LIKE YOU - IN FECT, I LIKE YOU SO MUCH I'M GOING TO MARRY YOU! YES BABY - I WANT YOU TO FLICK THE FLIES OFF MY TOP HET! WHAT DO YOU SAY??

I...I...I...GAH! ...ER, LISTEN, WHY DON'T I GO AND SLIP INTO SOMETHING MORE COMFORTABLE??

1368

AND SO:

STONE THE CROWS!! IT'S...IT'S...IT'S WHATSERNAME! MADAM!!! I HED NO IDEA YOU WERE EVEN IN THE CANTRY!!

DON'T GET UP - I'M ON A DISCREET PERSONAL FACT-FINDI MISSION!!

KING SMILING TOM GOODVIBES XXIII IS ENTERTAINING A VERY IMPORTANT PERSONAGE:

YOUR WHITENESS!! THIS IS INDEED AN HONOUR! I MUST GET OUT OF MY SEAT AND WILCOME YOU PROPER!

NO! NO! - IT'S ALRIGHT, DON'T GET UP!!

© STEVE BELL 1986

WILCOME TO THE LEND OF SEA, SUN, SURF AND SIPARATE DIVILOPMENT!! - WILCOME TO OUR BEAUTIFUL BEACHES, OUR LAVLY SAFARI POKS!!

AAAARRGH!

RUMBLE

THANKS TO SOMEBODY OR OTHER

SORRY ABOUT THIS, YOUR WHITENESS - THE OLD SPARE TYRE'S A BIT OUT OF CONTROWEL AT THE MOMENT!!!

ROLL

CRUNCH!

ANYWAY, I TRUST THAT THIS PUTS PAID ONCE AND FOR ALL TO ANY COMMUNIST PROPAGANDA ABOUT STARVATION IN THE TRIBAL HOMELENDS!

1369

36

40

41

42

43

46

47

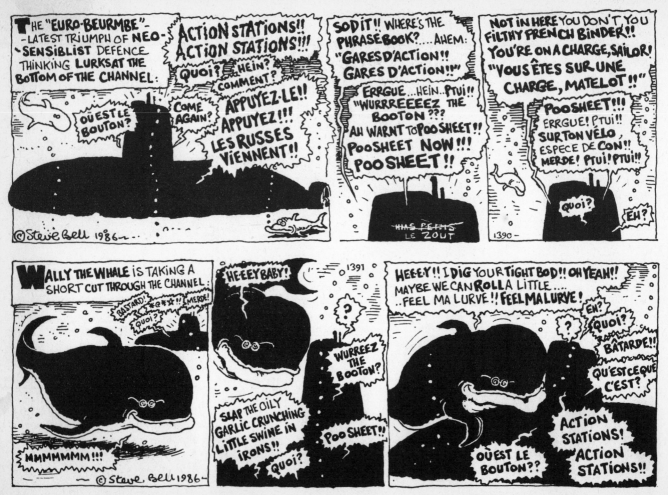

48

49

50

AT LAST: IN SEARING BLACK AND WHITE : SELECTED EXTRACTS FROM THE **BOOK** THEY TRIED TO MAKE **COMPULSORY** FOR UNSUSPECTING **SCHOOLCHILDREN**. AS TRANSLATED DIRECTLY FROM THE **ORIGINAL NORWEGIAN** :

© STEVE BELL 1986

Edwina lives with Norman and Kenneth

THANKS TO ANDY N.

Edwina lives in London. She is as old as her neck and slightly older than her teeth.

She lives with her spiritual father Norman, who is a practising Conservative.

He cohabits with Kenneth, a self confessed wet.

Some men fall in love with women and live together, some men fall in love with other men and live together. Some women fall in love with other women and live together. Some men or women fall in love with their money and gather together in mutual support groups.

We call these last sort of people Conservative politicians.

APOLOGIES TO SUSANNE BÖSCHE   1396.

Edwina lives with Norman and Kenneth

IT IS TUESDAY MORNING: EDWINA, NORMAN AND KENNETH ARE STAYING BY THE SEASIDE:

1397

Edwina bursts into the room shouting happily: "Up and out of your coffin, Norman! You too, Kenneth!" Norman grins indulgently. Kenneth, who always sleeps with his back to the wall with a bible strapped to his crotch, is a bit cross.

© STEVE BELL 1986

"Why can't you knock, Edwina?" he grumbles, "Look - if people see me and Norman sharing a room they might get the wrong end of the stick and think we're ....you know......"
— "You mean the stick you like to thrash children's bottoms with?" asks Edwina innocently.

51

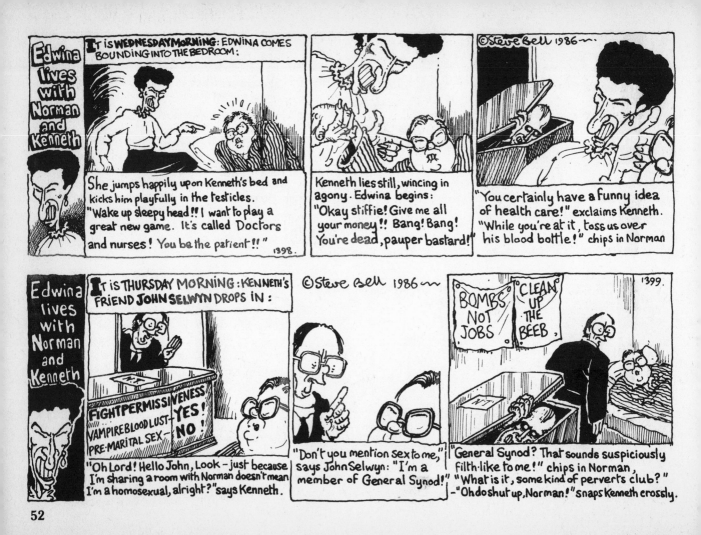

52

Edwina lives with Norman and Kenneth

IT IS FRIDAY MORNING. NORMAN IS UP AND OUT OF HIS COFFIN BRIGHT AND EARLY:

"Gosh, you're up early, Norman!" says Edwina, "What's going on?"

1400

"I can't stop 'ere chattering all day, girly, I gotta be orff to me unconsciousness raising group!" replies Norman, buttoning up his coat.

© Steve Bell 1986

"Unconsciousness-raising group? What on earth is that??" asks Edwina.

— "Well, basically, it's a regular event where me and a few chums get together and give the punters a bit of this:" says Norman, nutting the door down.

Edwina lives with Norman and Kenneth

IT IS SUNDAY MORNING: NORMAN, KENNETH + EDWINA ARE OFF TO CHURCH. ON THE WAY, A LOWER CLASS OLD LADY HURLS A GARLIC SANDWICH AT NORMAN:

"Why did she do that?" asks Edwina.

"She's frightened of us because she doesn't understand," Norman replies, "you see, she doesn't understand that as many as one in ten people are out, ..."

© Steve Bell 1986

"...practising, god bothering, conservative bloodsuckers like us. She doesn't think we should be allowed to flaunt it in public in this day and age. Don't worry, Edwina - she'll see reason ....."

1401

"...we'll just take away her pension!"

— "That's amazing," says Edwina, "where did you get that figure of one in ten??"

— "Oh that? I just made it up!" he replies.

— "I'm so glad I've got you, Norman!" beams Edwina happily.

54

55

56

58

59

60

61

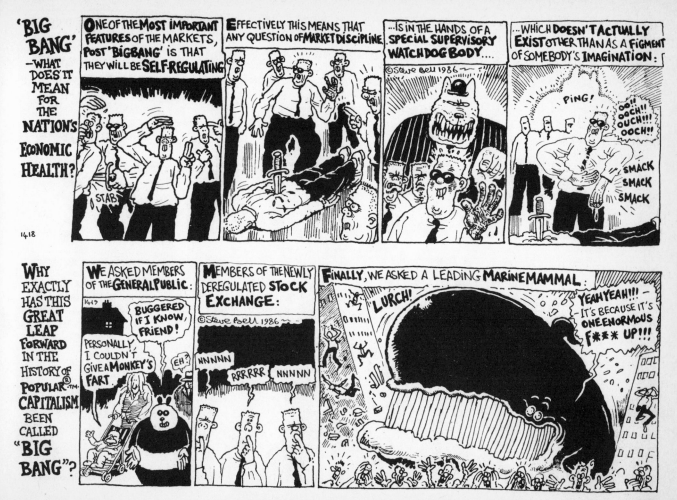

EARLY MORNING IN PECKHAM:

BLEURRRGH!! GREY NOVEMBER DAWN...

...SHALL I LEAP UP AND TAP DANCE ALL THE WAY TO THE KITCHEN TO MAKE A POT OF TEA, OR SHALL I REMAIN WHERE I AM AND HAVE A DISCREET SHERMAN?

CHOICES CHOICES...

HEY! DON'T YOU EVER KNOCK??

IMPORTANT LETTER FOR R. KIPLING ESQUIRE!

© Steve Bell 1986

AAAAAARRRGGHH!! NO!!! F*** MY OLD BOOTS!! I'VE BEEN SUMMONED FOR A 'RESTART' INTERVIEW! IT SAYS MY BENEFIT COULD BE AFFECTED IF I DON'T SHOW UP!!

CHOICES, CHOICES!

1420.

KIPLING IS ATTENDING HIS 'RESTART' INTERVIEW DOWN AT THE JOB CENTRE:

MR. R. KIPLING? PLEASE — TAKE A SEAT!!

© Steve Bell '86

I SEE FROM YOUR RECORDS THAT YOU'VE BEEN UNEMPLOYED FOR OVER FOUR YEARS NOW

1421.

LET'S GET ONE THING STRAIGHT — I'M NOT HERE TO HASSLE, I'M HERE TO TRY AND HELP YOU BY POINTING OUT A FEW EMPLOYMENT POSSIBILITIES YOU MAY NOT HAVE CONSIDERED YET

...YOU LOOK A BIT DOUBTFUL. YOU PROBABLY THINK I'M NOT SERIOUS, BUT I AM; I UNDERSTAND YOUR PREDICAMENT!

YOUR GOV'T NEEDS YOU OFF THE BOOKS

66

68

69

71

72

74

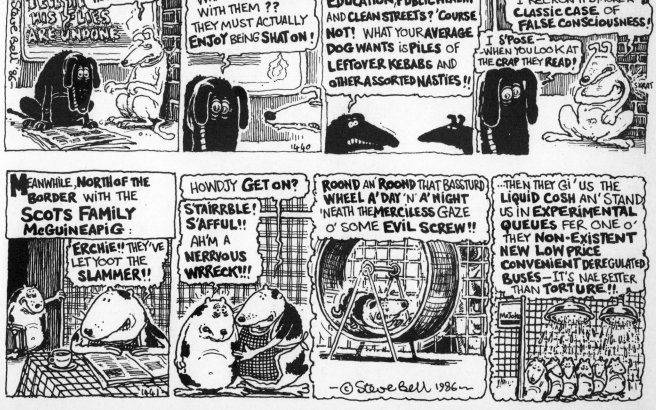

76

77

78

79

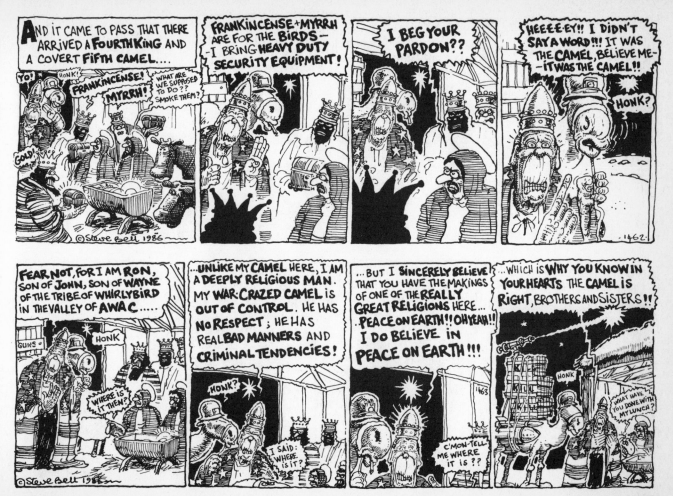

91

Introducing the
EXEMPLARY YOUTH ASSAULT SCHEME
with
EDDIE + MARK
© Steve Bell 1987
OK, HOLE-DIGGERS! THIS WAY TO THE WALL OF DEATH!!
OK! WE'VE GOT TO CLIMB UP THAT SHEER FACE AND BANG OUR HEADS ON THAT BELL AT THE TOP!!
1472
REMEMBER—THIS IS ABOUT TEAMWORK AND INITIATIVE! YOU - GO AND GET ME A PORTABLE TELEPHONE! YOU - GO AND GET ME A DECK-CHAIR!!
MUM? I WANT YOU TO GET SOMEONE TO SEND A HELICOPTER PRONTO!!

YOUTH TRAINING
WITH
MARK N' EDDIE
THANKS TO HEATHER
WHEN THE GOING GETS DICKY THE DICKS GET GOING....
WHUMPETY WHUMP WHUMP-A-WHUMP WHUMP-A
BOOST! BOOST! GO FOR IT!! BOOST!!!
1473
© Steve Bell 1987
JUNIOR! HOLEFORCE!! RAH! RAH! RAH!! WE'RE THE BOYS WHO WILL GO FAR!!
WHUMP WHUMP-A-
LOOK OUT WORLD!! IT'S MARK AND EDDIE! WE'RE TOUGH, WE'RE TIGHT! WE'RE ROUGH, WE'RE READY!! SO LET'S GET DIGGING!! JOIN OUR RANKS WE'RE RICH AS CRŒSUS THICK AS PLANKS!!
-WHUMPA- WHUMPA-

THIS is INCREDIBLE!
I'VE NEVER SEEN ANYTHING LIKE IT! I CANNOT SEE A THING!!
I CAN'T EVEN SEE YOU!
THESE ARE TOTAL SIBERIAN-STYLE WHITE-OUT WEATHER CONDITIONS!
WAIT A MINUTE! DID YOU SEE THAT?
NAH! IT WAS NOTHING- - JUST AN EXTRANEOUS INK SPOT! THIS is A GENUINE METEOROLOGICAL PHENOMENON!!
1478
14
©Steve Bell 1987

THESE SIBERIAN-STYLE TOTAL WHITE-OUT WEATHER CONDITIONS ARE JUST UNBELIEVABLE!! BUT WAIT! I THINK I SEE SOMETHING!! DOWN THERE! LOOK!!
NAH! THAT'S JUST A SIGNATURE!
YOU'RE RIGHT! IT'S GONE!!
LOOK! DO YOU SEE THAT? DOWN THERE! CLEAR AS ANYTHING!!
THAT'S THE STRIP NUMBER, YOU JERK!
IT'S INCREDIBLE HOW THEY CAN KEEP THEM COMING! I WOULDN'T LIKE TO BE OUT THERE WORKING IN THESE WEATHER CONDITIONS!
HEROIC, I CALL IT!!
©Steve Bell 1987
1479

97

Panel 1: THE SHIVERING SIBERIAN-STYLE WHITE-OUT WEATHER CONDITIONS CONTINUE UNABATED, BUT I'VE GOT A STRONG FEELING THAT WE'VE AT LAST REACHED THE CRUCIAL TRIGGER POINT FOR SEVERE WEATHER PAYMENTS!

HOW CAN YOU BE SO SURE?

1482

Panel 2: I'VE JUST SEEN ROY ROGERS!

WHAT DO YOU TAKE ME FOR?? WHAT WOULD ROY ROGERS BE DOING RIDING ROUND IN A SNOWSTORM HALFWAY UP THE PENNINES?

Panel 3: A FOWER-LAY-GED FRAY-UND ♪ A FOWER-LAY-GED FRAY-UND ♪....

STONE THE CROWS!! YOU WERE RIGHT! THERE HE GOES!!

Panel 4: — © Steve Bell 1987 —

STILL, TECHNICALLY SPEAKING, I SUPPOSE IT IS ABOUT AS LIKELY AS ANYONE EVER MEETING THE D.H.S.S. CRITERIA

Panel 5: SIBERIAN-STYLE ARCTIC-AGONY MOTORWAY-MADNESS TRAIN-TRAUMA WINTER-WONDERLAND WHITE-OUT WEATHER CONDITIONS CONTINUE UNABATED:

GASP! I THINK I'VE MADE IT AT LAST! IS THIS THE D.H.S.S.??

ERRM... MIGHT BE.... WHO'S ASKING?

1483

Panel 6: I'M A BONA FIDE O.A.P. SUFFERING GENUINE HARDSHIP

OH YES?

— © Steve Bell 1987 —

Panel 7: LOOK — I'VE IRREFUTABLE PROOF OF INABILITY TO COPE WITH HEATING COSTS FOR THE LAST THREE YEARS. SEE — ALL MY HEATING BILLS, ALL RECEIPTS FOR FOOD; CLOTHING + FOOTWEAR; LETTERS FROM THREE DOCTORS;

MMMMM

Panel 8: DEATH CERTIFICATE; BURIAL CERTIFICATE; LAST WILL AND TESTAMENT: SEE — NOT A SAUSAGE TO MY NAME! I'LL READ IT OUT TO YOU: "I BEQUEATH MY MAGIC TALKING TEETH TO THE D.H.S.S..."

OH YES... ...MMMM

98

99

100

104

108

110

112

113

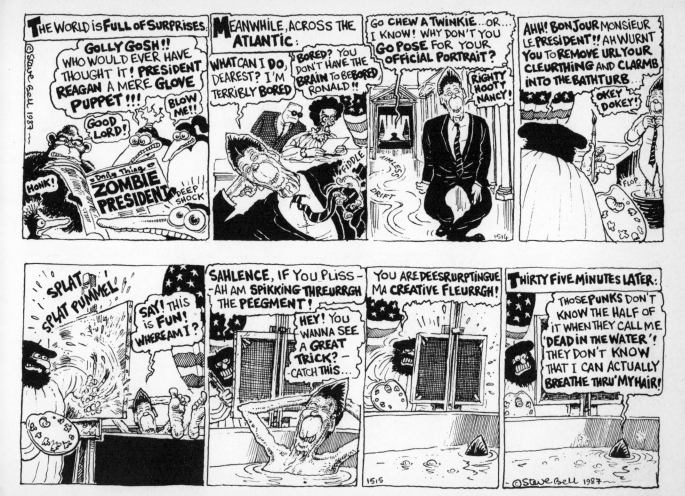

115

116

119

120

121

123

125

126

127

128

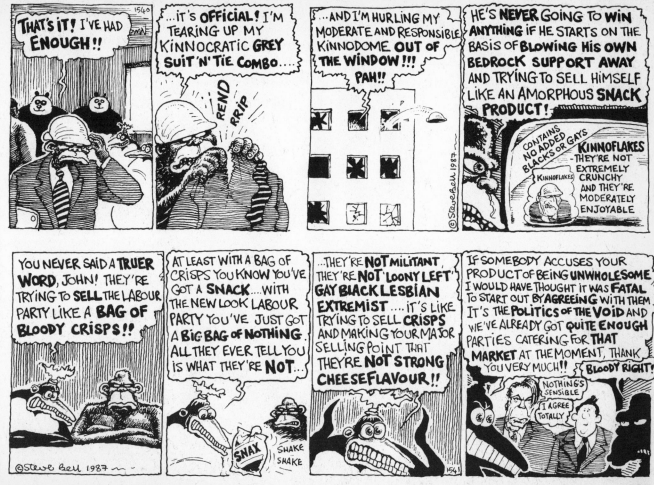

129

130

131

132

OKAY - I'VE DONE THE BABY, NOW GET ME A MONK!!
AAAAARRGHH AAAAARRGHH AARGGH!!!
SNAP
A MONK, MA'AM? ARE YOU SURE, MA'AM?
ANY PARTICULAR SORT OF MONK, MA'AM?
JUST GET ME A BLOODY MONK!
©Steve Bell 1987
BUT...BUT...BUT.... ...A MONK??
IT WORKED IN RUSSIA, IT CAN WORK IN FINCHLEY! GET ME A MONK NOW, AND MAKE IT SNAPPY!!
'548
EEK! WHERE ARE WE GOING TO FIND A SNAPPY MONK IN FINCHLEY AT THIS TIME OF NIGHT?!
OOOOER!!
OH DEAR! OOHDEAR!!

THATCHER'S BRITAIN 1987:
THIS IS ALL WE COULD FIND IN THE WAY OF A SNAPPY MONK, MA'AM. I THINK HE'S A BIT...YOU KNOW...THE WORSE FOR WEAR!
©Steve Bell 1987
I DON'T CARE - -JUST LEAN HIM UP AGAINST THAT CHURCH.. ...I'LL NEED A CANDLE!
OH GOD! A CANDLE!! HAVE WE GOT ANY CANDLES?
NO! NO CANDLES!
I'VE GOT A PACKET OF SPARKLERS...
HURRY UP, SCUM!!
HIC!
SHADDAP!
1549
THIS IS NO GOOD, YOU STUPID BASTARDS! GET ME ANOTHER BABY AND A DETACH-MENT OF SMILING SCHOOLCHILDREN!
EEK! EEK!
WHIMPER! WHIMPER!!
NNNNNN?

134

135

136

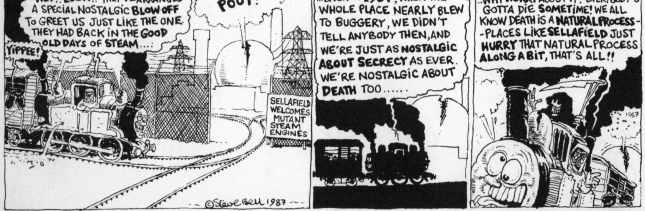

139

140

141

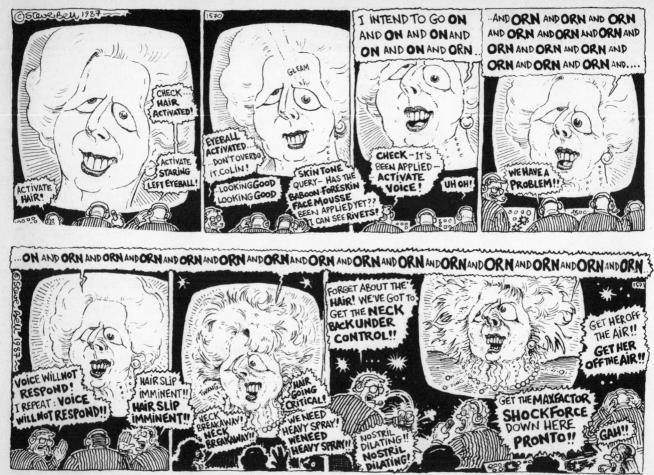

142

143

144

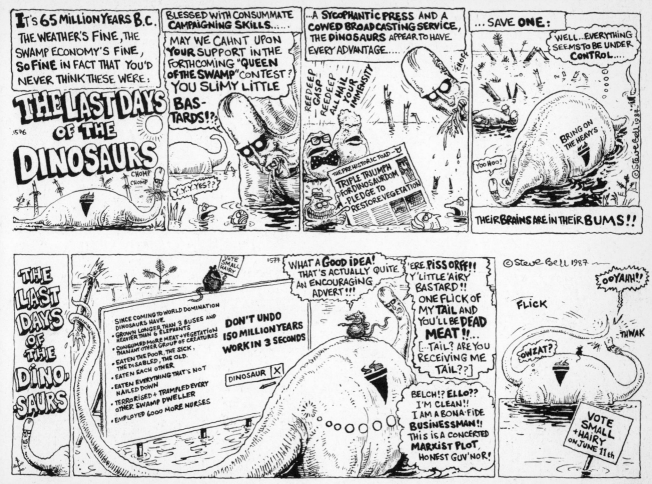

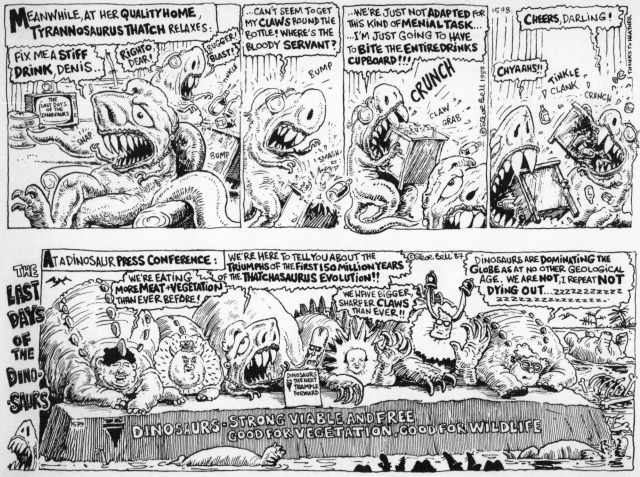

146

THE LAST DAYS OF THE DINOSAURS

DINOSAUR FREEDOM MEANS **REAL** FREEDOM. DINOSAUR FREEDOM MEANS THE **RIGHT** TO **OWN** YOUR OWN **SWAMP HOME** AND YOUR **OWN** SHARP SET OF TEETH! ...

TOPPLE!

DARLING I'M HOME!!

CRUSH

HELLO DARLING!

... DINOSAUR FREEDOM MEANS THAT YOUR **RIGHT** TO **PROVIDE** TASTY SNACKS IS FULLY PROTECTED UNDER THE **LAW**!!

OOYAH!!

DINOSAUR FREEDOM IS ABOUT **CHOICE**, FOR WITHOUT **CHOICE** THERE CAN BE **NO** FREEDOM AND WITHOUT **FREEDOM** THERE IS **NO FUTURE**:

DARLING! HOW ARE THE CHILDREN?

I'VE JUST EATEN THEM, DARLING! HERE – HAVE A PIECE OF QUALITY FURNITURE!!

NOW!

– © Steve Bell 1987

1580

THE LAST DAYS OF THE DINOSAURS

LET THE **SMALL HAIRIES** TAKE OVER? THET'S NOT AN **OPTION** – THET'S A **NIGHTMYAAH**!! ONLY **DINOSAURS** ARE **STRONG**! ONLY **DINOSAURS** ARE **VIABLE**!

SEE WHAT HEPPENS WHEN THE **SMALL HAIRIES** GRAB **CONTROL** OF LOCAL AREAS ....

SMALL GAY BLACK HAIRIES AGAINST GIANT LIZARDS

DINOSAURS OUT! OUT! OUT!

DINOSAUR FREE ZONE!

DINOSAUR FREE ZONE

1581

SEE THE **WRECKAGE**! SEE THE **DEVASTATION**!!

STOP DINOSAUR BALLROOM DANCING SESSIONS NOW!

SMALL HAIRINESS CANNOT **EVAH** WORK BECAUSE TO BE SMALL AND HAIRY IS TO BE **OUT OF DATE**, **DIMINUITIVE** AND **HIRSUTE**, AND ANYWAY, I'VE ABOLISHED IT!!

PHTNHARRRP!!

© Steve Bell 1987

148

149

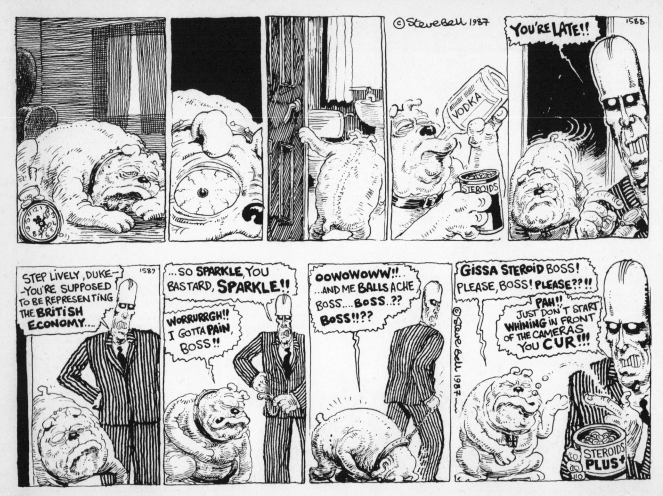

153

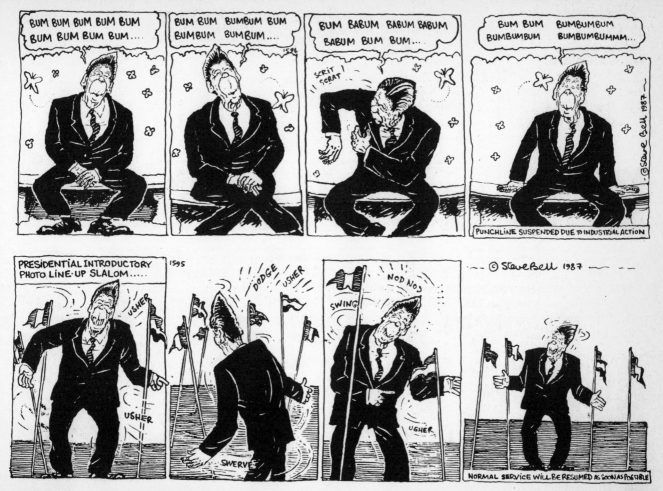

155

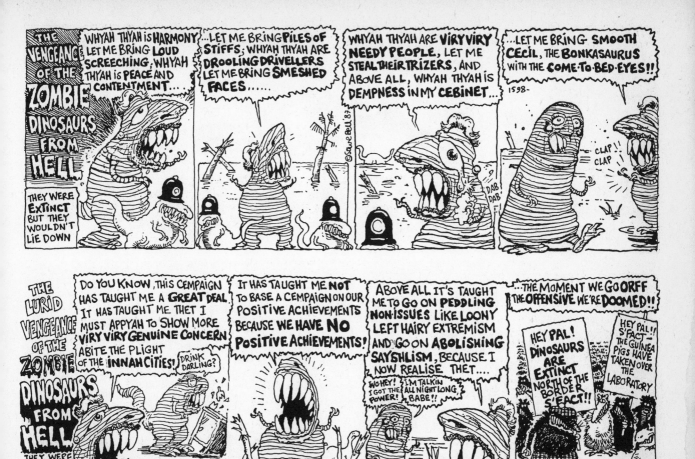

159

160